Religion, Science and Technology: An Orthodox Perspective

An Interview with Metropolitan Kallistos Ware
by MG Michael and Katina Michael

M&K Press
University of Wollongong, Australia

**Religion, Science and Technology:
An Eastern Orthodox Perspective**

Authors: Kallistos Ware
(with MG Michael and Katina Michael)
All rights reserved © 2017

Place: Wollongong, Australia
Printed by: M&K Press
Publisher: University of Wollongong
Year: 2017

978-1-74128-263-4 (paperback)
978-1-74128-264-1 (ebook)

Acknowledgement:
The interview with Kallistos Ware took place in Oxford, England on October 20, 2014. The interview was transcribed by Katina Michael and adapted again in Oxford on October 18, 2016 by Kallistos Ware himself in preparation for it to appear in print. MG Michael predominantly conceived the questions that framed the interview. Metropolitan Kallistos gave his consent and blessing for the adapted interview to be published in this format and reprinted as a feature interview in *IEEE Technology and Society Magazine*.

Online:
See www.mgmichael.com and www.katinamichael.com/interviews

Bibliography:

1. Technology. 2. Society. 3. Christian ethics – Eastern Orthodox.
4. Innovation. 5. Transhumanism. 6. Life and death.

Cover design by Katina Michael.
Cover graphic by MG Michael taken at Attali Monastery in Bali, Crete, Greece, 1984.

The Tower of Babel

11 Now the whole earth had one language and one speech. [2] And it came to pass, as they journeyed from the east, that they found a plain in the land of Shinar, and they dwelt there. [3] Then they said to one another, "Come, let us make bricks and bake them thoroughly." They had brick for stone, and they had asphalt for mortar. [4] And they said, "Come, let us build ourselves a city, and a tower whose top is in the heavens; let us make a name for ourselves, lest we be scattered abroad over the face of the whole earth." [5] But the Lord came down to see the city and the tower which the sons of men had built. [6] And the Lord said, "Indeed the people are one and they all have one language, and this is what they begin to do; now nothing that they propose to do will be withheld from them.

Genesis 11:1-6

Contents

A. Religion, Science and Technology 5
1. Difference between science and technology 6
2. Religion, science and technology 7
3. Are science and religion in conflict? 8
4. Abuses of technology in Judeo-Christian tradition 9
5. Technology practice in the ancient world 10
6. Technology's impact on our practise of religion ... 11

B. Creation, Innovation and Technological Progress 12
7. Image and likeness and trajectories of technology 13
8. Responsible innovation and scientific enquiry versus hubris .. 14
9. The Tower of Babel and engineering 15
10. Are there limits to innovation? 16

C. Morality and Technology 17
11. Can technology be 'immoral'? 18
12. Is religious faith threatened by technology? 19

D. Mortality and Technology 20
13. Can singularitarianism become the new religion? 21
14. Transhumanism and posthumanism 22
15. Human enhancement and medical prosthesis 23
16. Consciousness and 'brain in a vat' 24
17. Machines and artificial intelligence 25
18. Humanoid machines 26
19. Human transplantation 27
20. Sustaining life 28

A. Religion, Science and Technology

1. Do you differentiate between the terms science and technology? And is there a difference between the terms in your eyes?

Science, as I understand it, is the attempt systematically to examine reality. So in that way, you can have many different kinds of science. Physical science is involved in studying the physical structure of the universe. Human science is examining human beings. Thus the aim of science, as I understand it, is truth. Indeed, the Latin term *scientia* means knowledge. So, then, science is an attempt through the use of our reasoning brain to understand the world in which we live, and the world that exists within us. Technology, as I interpret it, means applying science in practical ways, producing particular kinds of machines or gadgets that people can use. So science provides the basis for technology.

2. What does religion have to say on matters of science and technology?

I would not call religion a science, though some people do, because religion relies not simply on the use of our reasoning brain but it depends also on God's revelation. So religion is based usually on a sacred book of some kind. If you are a Christian that means the Bible, the Old and New Testaments. If you are a Muslim, then the Old Testament and the Quran. So science as such does not appeal to any outside revelation, it is an examination of the empirical facts before us. But in the case of religion, we do not rely solely on our reasoning brain but on what God has revealed to us, through Scripture and in the case of an Orthodox Christian, through Scripture and Tradition. Technology, is something we would wish to judge in the light of our religious beliefs. Not all of the things that are possible for us to do applying our scientific knowledge are necessarily good. Technology by itself cannot supply us with the ethical standards that we wish to apply. So then religion is something by which we assess the value or otherwise of technology.

3. **Could we go insofar as saying that science and religion could be in conflict? Or at least is there a point where they might become incompatible one with the other?**

   I do not believe that there is a fundamental conflict between science and religion. God has given us a reasoning brain, he has given us faculties by which we can collect and organise evidence. Therefore, fundamentally all truth is from God. But there might be particular ways of using science which on religious grounds we would think wrong. So there is not a fundamental conflict, but perhaps in practice a certain clash. Problems can arise when, from the point of view of religion, we try to answer questions which are not strictly scientific. It can arise when scientists go beyond the examination of evidence and form value judgements which perhaps could conflict with religion. I would see conflict arising, not so much from science as such in the pursuit of truth, but from scientism, by which I mean the view that methods of scientific enquiry necessarily answer all the questions that we may wish to raise. There may be areas where science cannot give us the answer. For example, do we survive death? Is there a future life? That is to me a religious question. And I do not think that our faith in a future life can be proved from science, nor do I think it can be disproved by science. Equally, if we say God created the world, we are making a religious statement that in my view cannot be proved or disproved by science. So religion and science are both pursuing truth but on different levels and by different methods.

re any principles or examples in the Judeo-Christian n which point to the uses and abuses of technology?

cious element in the Judeo-Christian tradition is respect for an person. We believe as Christians that every person is e value in God's sight. Each person is unique. God expects :h one of us something that he does not expect from anyone are not just repetitive stereotypes. We are each made in ;e and likeness of God, and we realise that likeness and ach in our own way. Humans are unique basically because ess freedom. Therefore we make choices. And these choices e personal to each one of us determine what kind of person Now, any technology which diminishes our personhood, which ; us as humans, this I see as wrong. For example, to interfere iple's brains by medical experimentation, I would see as Medicine which aims to enable our bodies and our minds to correctly, that clearly I would see as good. But experiments ? been done by different governments in the 20th century, by Communism or in Nazi Germany, that I would see as an technology because it does not show proper respect for rity of the human person. So this would be my great test- echnology is undermining our personhood? Clearly our has to be limited because we have to respect the freedom people. And therefore, much of politics consists of a delicate .... of one freedom against another. But technology should be used always to enhance our freedom, not to obliterate it.

5. How did the ancient world generally understand and practise technology?

Interpreting technology in the broadest possible sense, I would consider that you cannot have a civilised human life without some form of technology. If you choose to live in a house that you have built yourself or somebody else has built for you, instead of living in a cave, already that implies a use of technology. If you wear clothes woven of linen, instead of sheepskins or goatskins, that again is a use of technology. In that sense, technology is not something modern, it came into existence as soon as people began using fire and cooking meals for themselves, for example. Clearly, the amount of technology that existed in the ancient world was far less than what we have today. And most of the technological changes have come, I suppose, in the last 200 years: the ability to travel by railway, by car, and then by plane; the ability to use telephones and now to communicate through the Internet. All of this is a modern development. Therefore we have an elaboration of technology, far greater than ever existed in the ancient world. That brings both advantages and risks. We can travel easily and communicate by all kinds of new means. This in itself gives us the opportunity to do far more, but the advantages are not automatic. Always it is a question of how we use technology. Why do we travel quickly from place to place? What is our aim? When we communicate with the Internet, what is it that we are wishing to communicate to one another? So value judgements come in as to how we use technology. That we should use it seems to me fully in accordance with Christian tradition. But the more complex technology becomes, the more we can do through technology, the more questions are raised whether it is right to do these things. So we have a greater responsibility than ever people had in the ancient world, and we are seeing the dangers of misuse of our technology, in for example the pollution of the environment. For the most part the ecological crisis is due to the wrong use of our technological skills. We should not give up using those skills, but we do need to think much more carefully how and why we are using them.

6. **In what ways has technology impacted upon our practise of religion? Is there anything positive coming from this?**

One positive gain from technology is clearly the greater ease by which we can communicate. We can share our ideas far more readily. A huge advance came in the fifteenth century with the invention of printing. You no longer had to write everything out by hand, you could produce things in thousands of copies. And now of course a whole revolution that has come in through the use of computers, which again renders communication far easier. But once more we are challenged: we are given greater power through these technological advances, but how are we going to use this power? We possess today a knowledge that earlier generations did not possess, quantitative, information, technological and scientific facts that earlier ages did not have. But though we have greater knowledge today, it is a question whether we have greater wisdom. Wisdom goes beyond knowledge, and the right use of knowledge has become much more difficult. To give an example from bioethics. We can now interfere in the processes of birth in a way that was not possible in the past. I am by no means an expert here, but I am told that it is possible or soon will be for parents to choose the sex of their children. But we have to ask: Is it desirable? Is it right, from a Christian point of view, that we should interfere in the mystery of birth in this way? My answer is that parents should not be allowed to choose the sex of their child. This is going beyond our proper human responsibility. This is something that we should leave in the hands of God, and I fear that there could be grave social problems if we started choosing whether we would have sons or daughters. There are societies where girls are regarded as inferior, and in due course there might arise a grave imbalance between the sexes. That is just one illustration of how technology makes things possible, but we as Christians on the basis of the teaching of the church have certain moral standards, which say this is possible but is not the right thing to do. Technology in itself, indeed science in itself, cannot tell us what is right or wrong. We go beyond technology, and beyond the strict methods of science, when we begin to express value judgements. And where do our values come from? They come from our religious belief.

B. Creation, Innovation and Technological Progress

7. How are we to understand the idea of being created in the "image and likeness" of God in the pursuit of the highest levels and trajectories of technology?

There is no single interpretation in the Christian tradition of what is meant by the creation of the human person according to the image and likeness of God. But a very widespread approach, found for example among many of the Greek fathers, is to make a distinction between these two terms. Image on this approach denotes the basic human faculties that we are given; those things which make us to be human beings, the capacities that are conferred on every human. The image is as it were, our starting point, the initial equipment that we are all of us given. The likeness is seen as the end point. The likeness means the human person in communion with God, living a life of holiness. Likeness means sanctity. The true human being on this approach is the saint. We humans, then, are travellers, pilgrims, on a journey from the image to the likeness. We should think of the human nature in dynamic terms. Fundamental to our personhood is the element of growth. Now, the image then means that we possess the power of rational thinking, the power of speech, articulate language with which we can communicate with others; it means therefore reason in the broadest sense. More fundamentally, it means that we humans have a conscience, a sense of right or wrong, that we make moral decisions. Most fundamentally of all, the image means that we humans have God-awareness, the possibility to relate to God, to enter into communion with him through prayer. And this to me is the basic meaning of the image, that we humans are created to relate to God. There is a direction, an orientation in our humanness. We are not simply autonomous. The human being considered without any relationship to God is not truly human. Without God we are only subhuman. So the image gives us the potentiality to be in communion with God, and that is our true nature. We are created to live in fellowship and in communion with God the Creator. So the image means you cannot consider human beings simply in isolation, as self-contained and self-dependent but you have to look at our relationship with God. Only then will you understand what it is to be human.

8. At what point would theologians or ethicists reckon we have crossed the line from responsible innovation and scientific enquiry over into "hubris"?

As a Christian theologian, I would not wish to impose, as if from a higher authority, limits on scientific enquiry. As I said earlier, God has given us the power to understand the world around us. All truth comes from him. Christ is present in scientific enquiry, even if his name is not mentioned. Therefore, I do not seek in a theoretical way to say to the scientist: Thus far and no further. The scientist, using the methods of enquiry that he has developed, should continue his work unimpeded. One cannot say that any subject is forbidden for us to look at. But there is then the question: how do we apply our scientific knowledge? Hubris comes in when scientists go beyond their proper discipline and try to dictate how we are to live our lives. Morality does not depend solely on scientific facts. We get our values, if we are Christians, from our faith. Modern science is an honest enquiry into the truth. So long as that is the case, we should say to the scientist: please continue with your work. You are not talking about God, but God is present in what you are doing, whether you recognise that or not. Hubris comes in when the scientist thinks he can answer all the questions about human life. Hubris comes in when we think we can simply develop our technology without enquiring: is this a good or bad application of science?

9. Is that well-known story of the Tower of Babel from the Book of Genesis (Gen 11: 1-9) at all relevant with its dual reference to "hubris" and "engineering"?

Yes, that is an interesting way of looking at the story of the Tower of Babel. The story of the Tower of Babel is basically a way of trying to understand why it is that we humans speak so many different languages and find such difficulty in communicating with one another. But underlying the story of Babel exactly is an overconfidence in our human powers. In the story of the Tower of Babel, the people think that they can build a tower that will reach from earth to heaven. By the power of engineering they think they can bridge the gap between the human and the divine. And this exactly would be attributing to technology, to our faculty for engineering, something that lies beyond technology and beyond engineering. Once you are moving from the realm of factual reality to the realm of heaven, then you are moving into a different realm where we no longer depend simply on our own powers of enquiry and our own ability to apply science. So exactly, the story of the Tower of Babel is a story of humans thinking they have unlimited power, and particularly an unlimited power to unite the earthly with the heavenly, whereas such unity can only come through a recognition of our dependence on God.

10. Why cannot or should we not explore and innovate, and go as far as is humanly possible with respect to innovation, if we carry the seed of God's creative genius within us?

Yes, we carry the seed of God's creative genius within us, but on the Christian world view we humans are fallen beings and we live in a fallen world. Now, how the fall is interpreted in Christian tradition can vary, but underlying all understandings of the fall is the idea that the world that we live in has in some way or another gone wrong. There is a tragic discrepancy between God's purpose and our present situation. As fallen human beings, therefore, we have to submit our projects to the judgement of God. We have to ask, not only whether this is possible but whether this is in accordance with the will of God. That obviously is not a scientific or technological question. It is not a question of what is possible but of what is right. Of course, it is true that many people do not believe in God, and therefore would not accept what I just said about this being a fallen world. Nevertheless they too, even those who have no belief in God, have to apply a moral understanding to science and technology. I hope they would do this by reflecting on the meaning of what it is to be human, on the value of personhood. And I believe that in this field it is possible, for Christians and non-Christians, for believers and unbelievers, to find a large measure of common ground. At the same time, we cannot fully understand our limitations as fallen human beings without reference to our faith. So the cooperation with the non-believer only extends to a certain limited degree.

C. Morality and Technology

11. Can a particular technology, for instance hardware or software, be viewed as being 'immoral'?

One answer might be to say technology is not in itself moral or immoral. Technology simply tells us what is possible for us to do. Therefore, it is the use we make of technology that brings us to the question of whether a thing is moral or immoral. On the other hand, I would want to go further than that, to say that certain forms of technology might in themselves involve a misuse of humans or animals. I have grave reservations, for example, about experiments on animals by dissection. Many of the things that are done in this field fail to show a proper respect for the animals as God's creation. So, it is not perhaps just the application of technology that can be wrong but the actual technology itself, if it involves a wrong use of living creatures, humans or animals. Again, a technology that involves widespread destruction of natural resources, that pollutes the world round us, that too, I would say in itself is wrong, regardless of what this technology is being used for. Often it must be a question of balancing one thing against another. All technology is going to affect people, one way or another. But there comes a point where the effect is unacceptable because it is making this world more difficult for other humans to live in. It is making the world unsuitable for future generations to survive within. Thus, one cannot make a sharp distinction between the technology in itself and how we apply it. Perhaps the technology itself may involve a wrongful use of humans, animals or natural things; wrongful because it makes the world somehow less pleasant and less healthy for us to live in.

12. Is religious faith in any way threatened by technology?

If we assume a scientific approach, that assumes that humans are simply elaborate machines, and if we develop technologies which work on that basis, I do think that is a threat to our religious faith, because of my belief in the dignity and value of the human person. We are not simply machines. We have been given free will. We have the possibility to communicate with God. So in assuming that the human being is merely a machine, we are going far beyond the actual facts of science, far beyond the empirical application of technology, since this is an assumption with deep religious implications. Thus there can be conflict when science and technology go beyond their proper limits, and when they do not show respect for our personhood.

D. Mortality and Technology

13. Can technology itself become the new religion in its quest for singularitarianism - the belief in a technological singularity, where we are ultimately becoming machines?

Yes. If we assume that science and technology, taken together, can answer every question and solve every problem, that would be making them into a new religion, and a religion that I reject. But science and technology do not have to take that path. As before, I would emphasise we have to respect certain limits, and these limits do not come simply from science or technology. We have, that is to say, to respect certain limits on our human action. We can, for example, by technology, bring people's lives to an end. Indeed, today increasingly we hear arguments to justify euthanasia. I am not at all happy about that as a Christian. I believe that our life is in God's hands and we should not decide when to end it, still less should we decide when to end other people's lives. Here, then, is a very obvious use of technology, of medical knowledge, where I feel we are overstepping the proper limits because we are taking into our hands that which essentially belongs to God.

14. Can you comment about the modern day quest toward transhumanism or what is now referred to as posthumanism?

I do not know exactly what is meant by posthumanism. I see the human person as the crown and fulfilment of God's creation. Humans have uniqueness because they alone are made in the image and likeness of God. Could there be a further development in the process of evolution, whereby some living being would come into existence, that was created but on a higher level than us humans? This is a question that we cannot really answer. But from the religious point of view, speaking in terms of my faith as a Christian, I find it difficult to accept the idea that human beings might be transcended by some new kind of living creature. I note that in our Christian tradition we believe that God has become human in Christ Jesus. The second person of the Trinity entered into our human life by taking up the fullness of our human nature into Himself. I see the incarnation as a kind of limit that we cannot surpass and that will not be superseded. And so I do not find it helpful to speculate about anything beyond our human life as we have it now. But we are not omniscient. All I would say is that it will get us nowhere if we try to speculate about something that would transcend human nature. The only way we can transcend human nature is by entering ever more fully into communion with God, but we do not thereby cease to be human. Whether God has further plans of which we know nothing, we cannot say. I can only say that, within the perspective of human life as we know it, I cannot see the possibility of going beyond the incarnation of Christ.

15. **Is human enhancement or bodily amplification an acceptable practice when considered against medical prosthesis?**

    Human enhancement and bodily amplification are acceptable if their purpose is to enable our human personhood to function in a true and balanced way but if we use them to make us into something different from what we truly are, then surely they are not. Of course that raises the question of acceptable, what we truly are. Here the answer, as I have already said comes not from science but from our religious faith.

16. What if consciousness could ever be downloaded through concepts such as 'brain in a vat'?

[Sigh]. I become deeply uneasy when such things are suggested, basically because it undermines the fullness of our personhood. Anything which degrades living persons into impersonal machines is surely to be rejected and opposed.

17. In the opposite vein, what if machines were to achieve fully fledged artificial intelligence through advancement?

When I spoke of what it means for humans to be created in God's image, I mentioned as the deepest aspect of this that we have God-awareness. There is as it were in our human nature a God-shaped hole which only he can fill. Now perhaps robots, automatic machines, can solve intellectual problems, can develop methods of rational thought, but do such machines have a sense of right or wrong? Still more, do such machines have an awareness of God? I think not.

18. What is so unique about our spirit which we cannot imbue or suggest into future humanoid machines?

The uniqueness of the human person for me is closely linked with our possession of a sense of awe and wonder, a sense of the sacred, a sense of the divine presence. As human beings we have an impulse within us that leads us to pray. Indeed, prayer is our true nature as humans. Only in prayer do we become fully ourselves. And to the qualities that I just mentioned, awe, wonder, a sense of the sacred, I would add a sense of love. Through loving other humans, through loving the animals, and loving God, we become ourselves, we become truly human. Without love we are not human. Now, a machine however subtle does not feel love, does not pray, does not have a sense of the sacred, a sense of awe and wonder. To me these are human qualities that no machine, however elaborate, would be able to reproduce. You may love your computer but your computer does not love you.

19. Where does Christianity stand on organ donation and matters related to human transplantation? Are there any guidelines in the bioethics domain?

In assessing such questions as organ donations, heart transplants and the like, my criterion is: do these interventions help the human person in question to lead a full and balanced human life? If organ transplants and the like enhance our life, enable us to be more fully ourselves, to function properly as human beings, then I consider that these interventions are justified. So, the question basically is: is the intervention life enhancing? That would bring me to another point. As Christians we see this life as a preparation for the life beyond death. We believe that the life after death will be far fuller and far more wonderful than our life is at present. We believe that all that is best in our human experience, as we now know it, will be reaffirmed on a far higher level after our death. Since the present life is in this way a preparation for a life that is fuller and more authentic, then our aim as Christians is not simply to prolong life as long as we can.

20. Can you comment on one's choice to sustain life through the use of modern medical processes?

The question therefore arises about the quality of life that we secure through these medical processes. For example, I recall when my grandmother was 96, the doctors suggested that various things could be done to continue to keep her alive. I asked how much longer will they keep her alive and the answer was, well perhaps a few months, perhaps a year. And when I discovered that this meant that she would always have various machines inserted into her that would be pumping things into her, I felt this is not the quality of life that I wish her to have. She had lived for 96 years. She had lived a full and active life. I felt, should she not be allowed to die in peace without all this machinery interfering in her. If on the other hand, it were a question of an organ transplant, that I could give to somebody who was half her age, and if that afforded a prospect that they might live for many years to come, with a full and active existence, then that would be very different. So my question would always be, not just the prolonging of life but the quality of the life that would be so prolonged. I do not, however, see any basic religious objection to organ transplants, even to heart transplants. As long as the personality is not being basically tampered with, I see a place for these operations. Do we wish to accept such transplants? That is a personal decision which each one is entitled to make.

Biographical Notes

Born Timothy Ware in Bath, Somerset, England, Metropolitan Kallistos was educated at Westminster School (to which he had won a scholarship) and Magdalen College, Oxford, where he took a Double First in Classics as well as reading Theology. In 1958, at the age of 24, he embraced the Orthodox Christian faith (having been raised Anglican), traveling subsequently throughout Greece, spending a great deal of time at the Monastery of St. John the Theologian in Patmos. He also frequented other major centers of Orthodoxy such as Jerusalem and Mount Athos. In 1966, he was ordained to the priesthood and was tonsured as a monk, receiving the name Kallistos. In the same year, he became a lecturer at Oxford, teaching Eastern Orthodox Studies, a position which he held for 35 years until his retirement. In 1979, he was appointed to a Fellowship at Pembroke College, Oxford, and in 1982, he was consecrated to the episcopacy as a titular bishop with the title Bishop of Diokleia, appointed to serve as the assistant to the bishop of the Ecumenical Patriarchate's Orthodox Archdiocese of Thyateira and Great Britain. Despite his elevation, Kallistos remained in Oxford and carried on his duties both as the parish priest of the Oxford Greek Orthodox community and as a lecturer at the University. Since his retirement in 2001, Kallistos has continued to publish and to give lectures on Orthodox Christianity, traveling widely. Until recently, he was the chairman of the board of directors of the Institute for Orthodox Christian Studies in Cambridge. On March 30, 2007, the Holy Synod of the Ecumenical Patriarchate elevated the Diocese of Diokleia to Metropolis and Bishop Kallistos to Titular Metropolitan of Diokleia.

Metropolitan Kallistos of Diokleia

Biographical Notes

Katina Michael and MG Michael

MG Michael and Katina Michael have been formally collaborating on technology and society issues since 2002. MG Michael holds a PhD in theology and Katina Michael in information and communication technology. Together they hold eight degrees in a variety of disciplines including Philosophy, Linguistics, Ancient History, Law and National Security. Presently, MG Michael is an honorary associate professor in the School of Computing and Information Technology at the University of Wollongong, and Katina Michael is a professor in the Faculty of Engineering and Information Sciences in the same institution, where she is also the Associate Dean (International). Since 2006, Michael and Katina have convened the annual *Social Implications of National Security* workshop, they have also written and edited six books, guest edited special issues of peer reviewed journals, and written widely on technological trajectories for the Institute of Electrical and Electronics Engineers. Katina is the editor-in-chief of *IEEE Technology and Society Magazine*, and senior editor of *IEEE Consumer Electronics Magazine*. Michael and Katina married in 1994 and reside in the Illawarra region in Australia with their three children.

Selected Works

Timothy Ware, *The Orthodox Church: An Introduction to Eastern Christianity*, Pelican Original, Harmondsworth: Penguin Books, 1963.

Timothy Richard Ware, *Eustratios Argenti: A Study of the Greek Church under Turkish Rule*, Oxford: Clarendon Press, 1964.

Igumen Chariton (Compiled by), E. Kadloubovsky (Translator), E.M. Palmer (Translator), Timothy Ware (Ed.), *The Art of Prayer: An Orthodox Anthology*, London: Faber and Faber, 1966.

Kallistos Ware, *The Orthodox Way*, London & Oxford: A.R. Mowbray & Co./ Crestwood, NY: SVS Press, 1979.

Saint Nicodemus the Hagiorite and Saint Makarios of Corinth (trans G.E.H. Palmer, Philip Sherrard, Kallistos Ware), *The Philokalia*, London, Boston: Faber and Faber, 1979, 1981, 1984, 1995.

Kallistos Ware, Thomas Hopko et al., *Women and the Priesthood*, Crestwood, NY: SVS Press, 1983.

Kallistos Ware, *The Power of the Name: The Jesus Prayer in Orthodox Spirituality*, Fairacres, Oxford: SLG Press, 1986.

Lev Gillet, Kallistos Ware, *The Jesus Prayer*, Crestwood, NY: SVS Press, 1987.

Kallistos Ware, Daniel J. Sahas, *Act Out of Stillness: the Influence of Fourteenth-Century Hesychasm on Byzantine and Slav Civilization*, Toronto: Hellenic Canadian Association of Constantinople and the Thessalonikean Society of Metro Toronto, 1995.

Kallistos Ware and Philip Sheldrake, *Spirituality: Eastern and Western Perspectives*, Cambridge: Great St Mary's, 1995.

Kallistos Ware, *How Are We Saved? The Understanding of Salvation in the Orthodox Tradition*, Minneapolis, Minnesota: Light & Life Publications, 1996.

Kallistos Ware, *The Inner Kingdom: Volume 1 of the Collected Works*, Crestwood, NY: SVS Press, 2000.

Elisabeth Behr-Sigel and Kallistos Ware, *The Ordination of Women in the Orthodox Church*, Geneva: WCC Publications, 2000.

Selected Works

Kallistos Ware, John Behr, Andrew Louth, and Dimitri E. Conomos, *Abba: the Tradition of Orthodoxy in the West*, Crestwood, NY: SVS Press, 2003.

Trans. G.E.H. Palmer, Philip Sherrard and Kallistos Ware, *Philokalia: The Eastern Christian Spiritual Texts: Selections, Annotated & Explained*, Woodstock, Vermont: Skylight Paths Publishing, 2006.

Kallistos Ware, *Orthodox Theology in the Twenty-First Century (Doxa & Praxis)*, WCC, 2012.

Online Lectures

Kallistos Ware, "Silence and glory: the message of St. Gregory Palamas for the world today", *OTV: Ohio State University*, https://www.youtube.com/watch?v=diizpNIUIqc, Last Accessed: April 9, 2002.

Kallistos Ware, "What is prayer?" *2008 Alfred S. Palmer Lecture Chapel*, Seattle Pacific University, https://www.youtube.com/watch?v=AqTLTUxMGbQ, Last Accessed: March 4, 2008.

Kallistos Ware, "Mystical theology of the Fathers", *OLTV: Orientale Lumen: Light of the East: An Eastern Christian Television Network*, https://www.youtube.com/watch?v=8kW0JSPbuSY, Last Accessed: January 15, 2010.

Kallistos Ware, "Salvation in Christ – The Orthodox Approach?" *2008 Alfred S. Palmer Lecture*, Seattle Pacific University, https://www.youtube.com/watch?v=3F7h-TStNd8, Last Accessed: May 9, 2012.

Kallistos Ware, "How should we study theology?" *2008 Alfred S. Palmer Lecture Theology Student Union Luncheon*, Seattle Pacific University, https://www.youtube.com/watch?v=rd0TNFSLipM, Last Accessed: August 19, 2012.

Kallistos Ware, "Conversation with Kallistos Ware", *Greek Orthodox Church goarch.org*, https://www.youtube.com/watch?v=pxatVu5Qi3k, Last Accessed: November 6, 2012.

Kallistos Ware, "From light to darkness: the Christian journey strangely reversed", *Institute for Orthodox Christian Studies Cambridge*, https://www.youtube.com/watch?v=boVsO7Xy8SE&t=145s, June 22, 2013.

Kallistos Ware, "Not ethnic but global: Orthodoxy in the western world", *Pemptousia, IOCS Community Lecture Day*, http://pemptousia.com/video/metropolitan-kallistos-ware-not-ethnic-but-global-orthodoxy-in-the-western-world/, February 22, 2014.

Kallistos Ware, "What does it mean to be a person? Parts 1-2", *Institute for Orthodox Christian Studies Cambridge*, https://www.youtube.com/watch?v=kV1QoD6LVcE, February 28, 2015.

Kallistos Ware, "St. Seraphim of Sarov", *OLTeleVision*, https://www.youtube.com/watch?v=x7BvFEQhCrI, March 7, 2015.

Kallistos Ware, "The unchanging gospel in an ever-changing culture", *North Park University: Engaging Orthodoxy Speaker's Series*, https://www.youtube.com/watch?v=6w8QQX1B71k, Last Accessed: March 5, 2016.

Index

advances 11
ancient 10
artificial intelligence 25
awareness 13, 25
bioethics 11, 27
brain 6-9, 24
children 11
choice 9
christ 14, 22
Christian 7, 9-11, 13-14, 16, 21-22, 27
communism 9
communicate 10-11, 13, 19
communion 13, 22
computer 11, 26
conflict 8, 19
conscience 13
consciousness 24
death 8, 27
dependence 15
earth 3, 15,
ecological 10
engineering 15
enhancement 23
euthanasia 21
faith 14, 16, 19, 22-23
fallen beings 16
freedom 9

gadgets 6
genesis 3, 15
generations 11, 18
God 7-9, 11, 13-16, 18-19, 21-22, 25-26
heart 27
hubris 14, 15
humans 9, 13, 15-16, 18-19, 22, 25-26
Incarnation 15, 22,
Judeo-Christian 9
judgement 9-11, 16
image and likeness 9, 13, 16, 22
immoral 18
impact 11
innovation 14, 16, 18
internet 10, 18
knowledge 6-7, 11, 14, 21
life 8, 10, 13-14, 21-22, 27
limits 14, 19, 21
love 26
machines 6, 19, 21, 24-27
medical 9, 21, 23, 27
methods 8, 11, 14, 25
misuse 10, 18
modern 10, 14, 22
moral 11, 13, 16, 18
morality 14
mortality 20
mystery 11

Nazi 9
omniscient 22
organ donation 27
Orthodox 7
person 13, 16, 19, 22-24, 26-27
personality 27
pollution 10
positive 11
posthumanism 22
power 11, 13-15
prayer 13, 26
prosthesis 23
quality 27
Quran 7
reality 6, 15
relationship 13
religion 7-8, 11, 21
responsible 14
right 10-11, 13, 16
robots 25
saint 13
sanctity 13
science 6-8, 11, 14-15, 19, 21, 23
scientia 6
scientific 7-8, 11, 14, 16, 19
Scripture 7
singularity 21
social problems 11
spirit 26
stereotypes 9

technology 6-7, 9-11, 13-16, 18-19, 21
telephones 10
tradition 7, 9-10, 13, 16, 22
transplants 27
Tower of Babel 3
trajectories 13
transhumanism 22
transplantation 27
travel 10, 13
truth 6, 8, 14,
uniqueness 22, 26
values 11, 14
wisdom 11
wrong 8-11, 13, 16, 18, 25

Notes

CPSIA information can be obtained
at www.ICGtesting.com
Printed in the USA
LVHW07n1447090818
586496LV00019B/451/P